To

Gina Erigero
....

From

Aunt Sany + the LaPoints
....
'This is for your new journey'

You are an amazing child of God,
precious to Him in every way. As you seek Him,
He will show you the mysteries of life
and unfold His unique plans for you—
a life full of rich blessings and delight.

Wherever your journey may take you,
God is right there with you. He is as close as breathing.
Let this journal inspire you to express your thoughts,
embrace your dreams, record your prayers,
and listen to what God is saying to you.

Your promises have been thoroughly tested;
that is why I love them so much.
PSALM 119:140 NLT

GOD'S PROMISES
FOR A
Girl's
HEART

*Ellie
Claire*
gift & paper expressions

...inspired by life

Beauty

✿ ✿ ✿

A woman of beauty...knows in her quiet center where God
dwells that He finds her beautiful, and deems her worthy,
and in Him, she is enough.

JOHN AND STASI ELDREDGE

My cup brims with blessing.
Your beauty and love chase after me
every day of my life.

PSALM 23:5–6 MSG

You can take no credit for beauty at sixteen.
But if you are beautiful at sixty,
it will be your soul's own doing.

MARIE CARMICHAEL STOPES

*You should clothe yourselves instead
with the beauty that comes
from within, the unfading beauty
of a gentle and quiet spirit,
which is so precious to God.*

1 PETER 3:4 NLT

June 25, 2013

I've never been the kind of person to keep a diary or a journal, even though I wish to become a writer someday. I guess I've just never had the time to write everyday about what happens to me during the day; I saw no purpose for it. This is why this book will not serve the useless purpose to be some silly diary where a pubescent teenage girl can write about how hard her life is. No, this book will be filled with the thoughts and feelings of a young woman, who wishes her life was just a bit more like a fictional story. I am that "young woman". My name is Gina Alicia Erigero. I was born on the 21st of January in the year 1999. I was adopted at birth by Greg and Dana Erigero. They have always been my parents; no one else. I am a 14 year old girl about to start high school, and this is my life story.

Eternal Life

✻ ✻ ✻

I have written these things to you who believe in the name of
the Son of God, so that you may know that you have eternal life.

1 JOHN 5:13 HCSB

If you are a believer, your judgment will not determine
your eternal destiny. Christ's finished work on Calvary
was applied to you the moment you accepted Christ as Savior.

BETH MOORE

Pursue righteousness, godliness, faith, love, endurance
and gentleness. Fight the good fight of the faith. Take hold of the
eternal life to which you were called when you made your good
confession in the presence of many witnesses.

1 TIMOTHY 6:11–12 NIV

*The gift of God is eternal life, spiritual life,
abundant life through faith in Jesus Christ,
the Living Word of God.*

ANNE GRAHAM LOTZ

Let me describe myself. I am 5 ft 8 ¾ and around 160 lbs. I choose not to weigh myself for I fear I would become self-conscience about my body. I live in Novato, California but was born in Spokane, Washington. I went to Our Lady of Loretto School from Kindergarten all the way through eigth grade. I will be attending Marin Catholic High School in August. My two best friends are Grace Beckman and Nikki Collier. Grace and I have been friends are entire lives. We are both adopted, and are moms went to high school together.

Blessings

✽ ✽ ✽

The sun...in its full glory, either at rising or setting—
this, and many other like blessings we enjoy daily;
and for the most of them, because they are so common,
most men forget to pay their praises.
But let not us.

IZAAK WALTON

And now, God, do it again—
bring rains to our drought-stricken lives
So those who planted their crops in despair
will shout hurrahs at the harvest,
So those who went off with heavy hearts
will come home laughing, with armloads of blessing.

PSALM 126:4–6 MSG

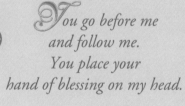

You go before me
and follow me.
You place your
hand of blessing on my head.

PSALM 139:5 NLT

Thoughts

✽ ✽ ✽

*Your thoughts are
the determining factor as to whose
mold you are conformed to.
Control your thoughts and you control
the direction of your life.*

CHARLES STANLEY

Search me, O God, and know my heart;
Try me and know my anxious thoughts;
And see if there be any hurtful way in me,
And lead me in the everlasting way.

PSALM 139:23–24 NASB

[Lord], preoccupy my thoughts
with Your praise beginning today.

JONI EARECKSON TADA

Know the God of your father, and serve Him
with a whole heart and a willing mind; for the LORD
searches all hearts, and understands every intent of the thoughts.
If you seek Him, He will let you find Him.

1 CHRONICLES 28:9 NASB

Prayer

✿ ✿ ✿

*O*ne single grateful thought raised to heaven
is the most perfect prayer.

G. E. LESSING

I love the LORD because he hears my voice
and my prayer for mercy.
Because he bends down to listen,
I will pray as long as I have breath!

PSALM 116:1–2 NLT

A prayerful heart and an obedient heart will learn,
very slowly and not without sorrow,
to stake everything on God Himself.

ELISABETH ELLIOT

*N*ever stop praying.

1 THESSALONIANS 5:17 NLT

Don't Worry

✻ ✻ ✻

*G*ive your cares to Him who cares for the flowers of the field.
Rest assured He will also care for you.

C. H. SPURGEON

*T*he minute I said, "I'm slipping, I'm falling,"
your love, God, took hold and held me fast.
When I was upset and beside myself,
you calmed me down and cheered me up.

PSALM 94:18–19 MSG

*W*orry is the senseless process of cluttering up tomorrow's
opportunities with leftover problems from today.

BARBARA JOHNSON

*D*o not worry about tomorrow,
for tomorrow will worry about itself.

MATTHEW 6:34 NIV

Plan A

❋ ❋ ❋

You can't start building a better tomorrow
if you wait till tomorrow to start building.

MARIE T. FREEMAN

"For I know the plans I have for you,"
declares the LORD, "plans to prosper you and not to harm you,
plans to give you hope and a future."

JEREMIAH 29:11 NIV

With God, it's never "Plan B" or "second best."
It's always "Plan A." And, if we let Him,
He'll make something beautiful of our lives.

GLORIA GAITHER

*Commit to the LORD whatever you do,
and your plans will succeed.*

PROVERBS 16:3 NIV

Created

✹ ✹ ✹

Christ is the visible image of the invisible God.
He existed before anything was created
and is supreme over all creation.

COLOSSIANS 1:15 NLT

God must've had a blast. Painting the stripes on the zebra,
hanging the stars in the sky, putting gold in the sunset.
What creativity.

MAX LUCADO

By Him all things were created, both in the heavens
and on earth, visible and invisible...all things
have been created through Him and for Him.

COLOSSIANS 1:16 NASB

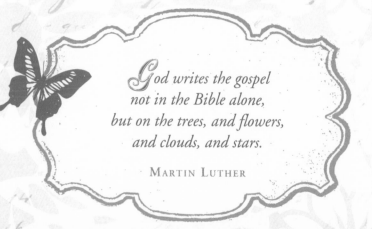

*God writes the gospel
not in the Bible alone,
but on the trees, and flowers,
and clouds, and stars.*

MARTIN LUTHER

Joy

✦ ✦ ✦

*G*od...richly provides us with everything for our enjoyment.

1 TIMOTHY 6:17 NIV

*T*he Christian lifestyle is not one of legalistic do's and don'ts,
but one that is positive, attractive, and joyful.

VONETTE BRIGHT

*The joy of the LORD
is your strength.*

NEHEMIAH 8:10 NIV

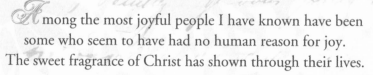

*A*mong the most joyful people I have known have been
some who seem to have had no human reason for joy.
The sweet fragrance of Christ has shown through their lives.

ELISABETH ELLIOT

*G*od's kingdom [is] what God does with your life as he
sets it right, puts it together, and completes it with joy.

ROMANS 14:17 MSG

On Hard Days

✻ ✻ ✻

We take the good days from God—why not also the bad days?

JOB 2:10 MSG

Stick through the hard times, one day you will laugh at them.

SHERRI M.

On a good day, enjoy yourself;
On a bad day, examine your conscience.
God arranges for both kinds of days
So that we won't take anything for granted.

ECCLESIASTES 7:14 MSG

Don't quit in hard times; pray all the harder.
Help needy Christians; be inventive in hospitality.

ROMANS 12:12 MSG

When times get hard, remember Jesus.
When people don't listen, remember Jesus.
When tears come, remember Jesus.

MAX LUCADO

Strength in Christ

✦ ✦ ✦

You can fight with confidence where you are sure of victory.
With Christ and for Christ victory is certain.

BERNARD OF CLAIRVAUX

God has said, "Never will I leave you;
never will I forsake you." So we say with confidence,
"The Lord is my helper; I will not be afraid.
What can man do to me?"

HEBREWS 13:5–6 NIV

Soldiers of Christ, arise,
And put your armor on,
Strong in the strength which God supplies
Through His eternal Son.

CHARLES WESLEY

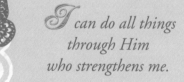

I can do all things
through Him
who strengthens me.

PHILIPPIANS 4:13 NASB

Thankful

✻ ✻ ✻

*Give thanks to the LORD,
for he is good;
his love endures forever.*

PSALM 118:1 NIV

*I*f we thank God for all the good things,
we won't have time to complain about the bad.

*T*hanks be to God for his indescribable gift!

2 CORINTHIANS 9:15 NIV

*W*ouldn't it make an astounding difference...if we recognized
God's gracious gift in every single task?

ELISABETH ELLIOT

*E*verything God created is good, and to be received
with thanks. Nothing is to be sneered at and thrown out.
God's Word and our prayers make every item in creation holy.

1 TIMOTHY 4:4 MSG

Sacrifice

* * *

I am the good shepherd.
The good shepherd lays down his life for the sheep.

JOHN 10:11 NIV

Live your lives in love, the same sort of love
which Christ gives us, and which He perfectly expressed
when He gave Himself as a sacrifice to God.

CORRIE TEN BOOM

I beseech you therefore...by the mercies of God,
that you present your bodies a living sacrifice, holy,
acceptable to God, which is your reasonable service.

ROMANS 12:1 NKJV

*Christian character
is the flower of which
sacrifice is the seed.*

FATHER ANDREW

Happiness

✺ ✺ ✺

It is pleasing to...God whenever you rejoice or laugh
from the bottom of your heart.

MARTIN LUTHER

Hallelujah! Happy is the [person] who fears the LORD,
taking great delight in His commandments.

PSALM 112:1 HCSB

If you want to be truly happy,
you won't find it on an endless quest for more stuff.
You'll find it in receiving God's generosity
and then passing that generosity along.

BILL HYBELS

*Laugh with your
happy friends when they're happy.*

ROMANS 12:15 MSG

Family & Home

* * *

> *I like to think of my family as a big,
> beautiful patchwork quilt—each of us so different yet
> stitched together by love and life experiences.*
>
> BARBARA JOHNSON

All of you should be of one mind.
Sympathize with each other. Love each other as brothers
and sisters. Be tenderhearted, and keep a humble attitude.

1 PETER 3:8 NLT

A home is a place where we find direction.

GIGI GRAHAM TCHIVIDJIAN

Each of you must respect his mother and father.

LEVITICUS 19:3 NIV

The Golden Rule starts at home,
but it should never stop there.

MARIE T. FREEMAN

Friends

If you have a gift for showing kindness to others, do it gladly. Don't just pretend to love others. Really love them.

ROMANS 12:8–9 NLT

How good and pleasant it is
when [we] live together in unity!

PSALM 133:1 NIV

Do you want to be wise? Choose wise friends.

CHARLES SWINDOLL

A friend is a person with a sneaky knack of saying good things about you behind your back.

MARILYN JANSEN

A sweet friendship refreshes the soul.

PROVERBS 27:9 MSG

Kindness

* * *

A person who really cares about his or her neighbor,
a person who genuinely loves others, is a person
who bears witness to the truth.

ANNE GRAHAM LOTZ

When you're kind to others, you help yourself;
when you're cruel to others, you hurt yourself.

PROVERBS 11:17 MSG

Friendships are glued together with little kindnesses.

MERCIA TWEEDALE

Since God chose you to be the holy people he loves,
you must clothe yourselves with tenderhearted mercy,
kindness, humility, gentleness, and patience.

COLOSSIANS 3:12 NLT

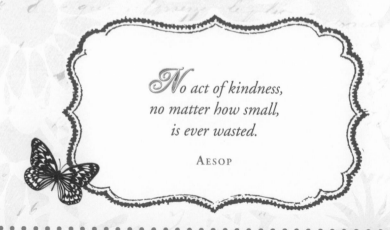

*No act of kindness,
no matter how small,
is ever wasted.*

AESOP

Word of God

✦ ✦ ✦

*L*ike newborn babies, long for the pure milk of the word,
so that by it you may grow in respect to salvation.

1 PETER 2:2 NASB

*T*here is no way to draw closer to God unless you are
in the Word of God every day. It's your compass. Your guide.
You can't get where you need to go without it.

STORMIE OMARTIAN

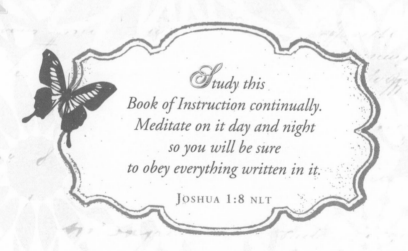

*S*tudy this
Book of Instruction continually.
Meditate on it day and night
so you will be sure
to obey everything written in it.

JOSHUA 1:8 NLT

*W*e're the only Bible some people may ever read,
so we're like walking, living, breathing Bibles.

ROBIN JONES GUNN

Faith

* * *

*Faith is being sure
of what we hope for
and certain of
what we do not see.*

HEBREWS 11:1 NIV

If God chooses to remain silent, faith is content.

RUTH BELL GRAHAM

I know the LORD is always with me.
I will not be shaken, for he is right beside me.

PSALM 16:8 NLT

No ray of sunshine is ever lost, but the green
which it awakes into existence needs time to sprout,
and it is not always granted to the sower to see the harvest.
All work that is worth anything is done in faith.

ALBERT SCHWEITZER

We live by faith, not by sight.

2 CORINTHIANS 5:7 NIV

Forgiveness

* * *

*Smart people know
how to hold their tongue;
their grandeur is to forgive and forget.*

PROVERBS 19:11 MSG

"Can you please forgive me for judging you?"...
I continued. "I was having some pretty bad thoughts toward you.
And now I'm sorry."

MELODY CARLSON

Be even-tempered, content with second place,
quick to forgive an offense. Forgive as quickly and completely
as the Master forgave you.

COLOSSIANS 3:13 MSG

One of the very best ways to let people know
we really love them is to say, and mean it: "I'm sorry I hurt you.
Please forgive me."

CHARLIE W. SHEDD

Be Cheerful

* * *

*B*e cheerful no matter what.

1 THESSALONIANS 5:16 MSG

*I*f we are cheerful and contented, all nature smiles...
the flowers are more fragrant, the birds sing more sweetly,
and the sun, moon, and stars all appear more beautiful,
and seem to rejoice with us.

ORISON SWETT MARDEN

*W*orry weighs us down; a cheerful word picks us up.

PROVERBS 12:25 MSG

*W*e may run, walk, stumble, drive, or fly, but let us
never lose sight of the reason for the journey, or miss a chance
to see a rainbow on the way.

GLORIA GAITHER

*B*cheerful heart
is good medicine,
but a crushed spirit
dries up the bones.

PROVERBS 17:22 NIV

Love

❋ ❋ ❋

For the LORD is good and his love endures forever;
his faithfulness continues through all generations.

PSALM 100:5 NIV

A bird does not know it can fly before it uses its wings.
We learn God's love in our hearts as soon as we act upon it.

CORRIE TEN BOOM

Let love be your highest goal!

1 CORINTHIANS 14:1 NLT

Let's not pray long, drawn-out prayers,
but let's pray short ones full of love.

MOTHER TERESA

*Love God, your God,
with your whole heart: love him
with all that's in you,
love him with all you've got!*

DEUTERONOMY 6:5 MSG

Show It

Yes, just as you can identify a tree by its fruit,
so you can identify people by their actions.

MATTHEW 7:20 NLT

If we have the true love of God in our hearts, we will show it
in our lives. We will not have to go up and down the earth
proclaiming it. We will show it in everything we say or do.

BARBARA JOHNSON

In everything set them an example by doing what is good.

TITUS 2:7 NIV

Our words speak, but our actions speak much more loudly.
And whether we like it or not, all of us are role models.
Our friends and family members observe our actions;
as followers of Christ, we are obliged to act accordingly.

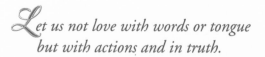

*Let us not love with words or tongue
but with actions and in truth.*

1 JOHN 3:18 NIV

Quietly

❋ ❋ ❋

Growth takes place in quietness, in hidden ways, in silence
and solitude. The process is not accessible to observation.

EUGENE PETERSON

Speak, for your servant is listening.

1 SAMUEL 3:10 NIV

The world is full of noise. Might we not set ourselves
to learn silence, stillness, solitude?

ELISABETH ELLIOT

*In quietness
and confidence
is your strength.*

ISAIAH 30:15 NLT

And so, for a refreshing change, I kept my mouth shut.

MELODY CARLSON

People will believe anything if you whisper it.

FARMER'S ALMANAC

Be Unique

✦ ✦ ✦

What we do is less than a drop in the ocean. But if that drop were missing, the ocean would lack something.

MOTHER TERESA

Let's just go ahead and be what we were made to be, without enviously or pridefully comparing ourselves with each other, or trying to be something we aren't.

ROMANS 12:6 MSG

No matter what some people may say, you are important. You. God loves even the weirdest parts of you. He knows that those parts have value you may not yet understand.

MARILYN JANSEN

All kinds of things are handed out by the Spirit, and to all kinds of people! The variety is wonderful.... All these gifts have a common origin, but are handed out one by one by the one Spirit of God. He decides who gets what, and when.

1 CORINTHIANS 12:4–5 MSG

Joyful Song

✿ ✿ ✿

*Joy is the heart's
harmonious response
to the Lord's song of love.*

A. W. TOZER

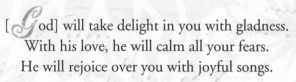

[God] will take delight in you with gladness.
With his love, he will calm all your fears.
He will rejoice over you with joyful songs.

ZEPHANIAH 3:17 NLT

When faith is strong, troubles become trifles.
There can be comfort in sorrow because
in the midst of mourning, God gives a song.

BILLY GRAHAM

Sing praises over everything, any excuse for a song
to God the Father in the name of our Master, Jesus Christ.

EPHESIANS 5:19 MSG

Talk

Let everything you say be good and helpful,
so that your words will be an encouragement
to those who hear them.

EPHESIANS 4:29 NLT

When you talk, choose the very same words that
you would use if Jesus were looking over your shoulder.
Because He is.

MARIE T. FREEMAN

*The mouth speaks out of that
which fills the heart.*

MATTHEW 12:34 NASB

There's an opportune time to do things,
a right time for everything on the earth.... A right time to shut up
and another to speak up.

ECCLESIASTES 3:1, 7 MSG

Dreams

* * *

*There is nothing
like a dream
to create the future.*

VICTOR HUGO

Dreams and goals help you go on in faith.

ASHLEY H.

Hope deferred makes the heart sick,
but a dream fulfilled is a tree of life.

PROVERB 13:12 NLT

No one's ever seen or heard anything like this,
Never so much as imagined anything quite like it—
What God has arranged for those who love him.

1 CORINTHIANS 2:9 MSG

Your future is as bright as the promises of God.

ADONIRAM JUDSON

He Helps Us

* * *

*I*t is only the first step that is difficult.

MARIE DE VICHY-CHAMROND

*W*hatever God tells us to do, He also helps us to do.

DORA GREENWELL

*I*f you have made mistakes...there is always
another chance for you.... You may have a fresh start
any moment you choose, for this thing we call "failure" is not
the falling down, but the staying down.

MARY PICKFORD

*I*f God is for us, who can be against us?

ROMANS 8:31 NIV

*G*od's Spirit is right alongside
helping us along. If we don't know how
or what to pray, it doesn't matter. He does
our praying in and for us, making prayer
out of our wordless sighs, our aching groans.

ROMANS 8:26 MSG

Trust

✤ ✤ ✤

> *Trust in the LORD*
> *with all your heart,*
> *And lean not on*
> *your own understanding.*
>
> PROVERBS 3:5 NKJV

We don't have to be perfect.... We are asked only to be real,
trusting in His perfection to cover our imperfection.

GIGI GRAHAM TCHIVIDJIAN

Trust in Him at all times, O people;
Pour out your heart before Him.

PSALM 62:8 NASB

How changed our lives would be if we could only fly
through the days on wings of surrender and trust!

HANNAH WHITALL SMITH

Blessed are those who trust in the LORD
and have made the LORD their hope and confidence.

JEREMIAH 17:7 NLT

Character

* * *

Don't lose a minute in building on what you've been given,
complementing your basic faith with good character,
spiritual understanding, alert discipline, passionate patience,
reverent wonder, warm friendliness, and generous love,
each dimension fitting into and developing the others.

2 PETER 1:5–6 MSG

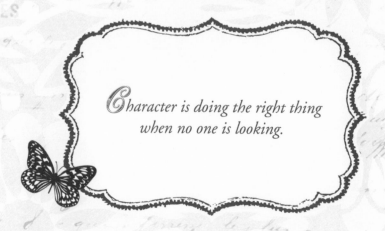

*Character is doing the right thing
when no one is looking.*

God-loyal people, living honest lives,
make it much easier for their children.

PROVERBS 20:7 MSG

Do nothing that you would not like to be doing
when Jesus comes. Go no place where you would
not like to be found when He returns.

CORRIE TEN BOOM

Never Quit

✽ ✽ ✽

*A*nyone who doesn't make mistakes isn't trying hard enough.

WESS ROBERTS

*L*ove never gives up,
never loses faith, is always hopeful,
and endures through every circumstance.

1 CORINTHIANS 13:7 NLT

*W*hen life becomes all snarled up, offer it to our Lord
and let Him untie the knots.

MARILYN JANSEN

*L*et us throw off everything that hinders and the sin
that so easily entangles, and let us run with perseverance
the race marked out for us. Let us fix our eyes on Jesus,
the author and perfector of our faith.

HEBREWS 12:1–2 NIV

*N*ever, Never, Never Quit.

WINSTON CHURCHILL

A Happy Heart

✿ ✿ ✿

Look at how great a love the Father has given us,
that we should be called God's children. And we are!

1 JOHN 3:1 HCSB

*A happy heart
is the best service
we can give to God.*

MARIE CHAPIAN

Light dawns for the righteous,
gladness for the upright in heart.
Be glad in the LORD, you righteous ones,
and praise His holy name.

PSALM 97:11–12 HCSB

Our hearts are not made happy by words alone.
We should seek a good and pure life, setting our minds at rest
and having confidence before God.

THOMAS À KEMPIS

Joyful Heart

✿ ✿ ✿

*A joyful heart
makes a cheerful face,
but when the heart is sad,
the spirit is broken.*

PROVERBS 15:13 NASB

A joyful heart is like a sunshine of God's love,
the hope of eternal happiness, a burning flame of God....
And if we pray, we will become that sunshine of God's love—
in our own home, the place where we live,
and in the world at large.

MOTHER TERESA

My servants shall sing for joy of heart.

ISAIAH 65:14 KJV

A joyful heart is life itself, and rejoicing lengthens one's life.

ECCLESIASTICUS

God Is Good

* * *

> *Lovely flowers
> are the smiles
> of God's goodness.*
>
> WILLIAM WILBERFORCE

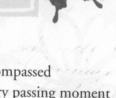

Those who love God are encompassed
with gladness on every side, because in every passing moment
they see and feel the Father's love, and nothing of this world
can take it away or lessen it.

H. L. SIDNEY LEAR

God is good to one and all;
everything he does is suffused with grace.

PSALM 145:9 MSG

Our God is so wonderfully good, and lovely, and blessed
in every way that the mere fact of belonging to Him is enough
for an untellable fullness of joy!

HANNAH WHITALL SMITH

A Cheerful Giver

* * *

To those who use well what they are given,
even more will be given, and they will have an abundance.

MATTHEW 25:29 NLT

If it's nothing more than a smile—
give that away and keep on giving it.

BETH BROWN

Each of us has something different to contribute,
and no matter how small or insignificant it may seem,
it can be for the benefit of all.

LAURITZ MELCHIOR

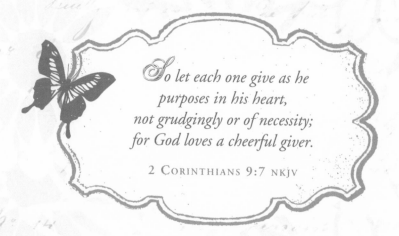

So let each one give as he
purposes in his heart,
not grudgingly or of necessity;
for God loves a cheerful giver.

2 CORINTHIANS 9:7 NKJV

Wisdom

· · ·

*Even the angels—
as full of wisdom
as they are—
don't know everything.*

EILEEN ELIAS FREEMAN

Don't turn your back on wisdom, for she will protect you.
Love her, and she will guard you.
Getting wisdom is the wisest thing you can do!
And whatever else you do, develop good judgment.

PROVERBS 4:6–7 NLT

The more wisdom enters our hearts, the more we will be able
to trust our hearts in difficult situations.

JOHN ELDREDGE

Those who are wise will shine like the brightness
of the heavens, and those who lead many to righteousness,
like the stars for ever and ever.

DANIEL 12:3 NIV

Temptation

* * *

*You are less likely
to fall into temptation
if you don't walk along the edge.*

BRUCE BICKEL AND STAN JANTZ

Life is a series of choices between the bad, the good,
and the best. Everything depends on how we choose.

VANCE HAVNER

Keep a cool head. Stay alert. The Devil is poised to pounce,
and would like nothing better than to catch you napping.
Keep your guard up.

1 PETER 5:8 MSG

Because Christ has faced our every temptation without sin,
we never face a temptation that has no door of escape.

Finally...whatever is true, whatever is honorable,
whatever is right, whatever is pure, whatever is lovely,
whatever is of good repute...dwell on these things.

PHILIPPIANS 4:8 NASB

The Bright Side

✳ ✳ ✳

Try to keep your sense of humor! When you can see
the funny side of a problem, sometimes it stops
being so much of a problem.

EMILIE BARNES

Keep your face to the sunshine
and you cannot see the shadow.

HELEN KELLER

The ways of right-living people glow with light;
the longer they live, the brighter they shine.

PROVERBS 4:18 MSG

It never hurts your eyesight
to look on the bright side of things.

BARBARA JOHNSON

*In this world
you will have trouble.
But take heart!
I have overcome the world.*

JOHN 16:33 NIV

My Very Best

❁ ❁ ❁

Work willingly at whatever you do, as though
you were working for the Lord rather than for people.

COLOSSIANS 3:23 NLT

*I do the very best I know how—
the very best I can;
and mean to keep doing so until the end.*

ABRAHAM LINCOLN

If we did the things we are capable of,
we would astound ourselves.

THOMAS EDISON

Whatever your hand finds to do, do it with all your might.

ECCLESIASTES 9:10 NASB

Success or failure can be pretty well predicted by the degree
to which the heart is fully in it.

JOHN ELDREDGE

Humble Heart

✳ ✳ ✳

All of you, take up My yoke and learn from Me,
because I am gentle and humble in heart,
and you will find rest for yourselves.

MATTHEW 11:29 HCSB

The way of ascending is humility; the way of descending
is pride. If our heart is humble we shall be lifted to heaven.

BENEDICT OF NURSIA

Always be humble and gentle. Be patient with each other,
making allowance for each other's faults because of your love.

EPHESIANS 4:2 NLT

God will lift up all who have a humble spirit
and save them in all trials and tribulations.

THOMAS À KEMPIS

Don't be selfish;
don't try to impress others.
Be humble, thinking of others
as better than yourselves.

PHILIPPIANS 2:3 NLT

Comfort

* * *

[Jesus asked,] "Are you left out of things? Feeling rejected
and pushed aside? Come home to Me."

ALICE CHAPIN

For the LORD comforts his people and will
have compassion on his afflicted ones.

ISAIAH 49:13 NIV

Praise be to the God and Father of our Lord Jesus Christ,
the Father of compassion and the God of all comfort,
who comforts us in all our troubles, so that we can comfort
those in any trouble with the comfort we ourselves
have received from God.

2 CORINTHIANS 1:3–4 NIV

How comforting!
He knows me completely
and still loves me.

NEVA COYLE

Believe

✤ ✤ ✤

Because you have seen me,
you have believed;
blessed are those who have not seen
and yet have believed.

JOHN 20:29 NIV

---

*M*iracles happen to those who believe in them.

BERNARD BERENSEN

*A*nyone who wants to approach God must believe
both that he exists and that he cares enough
to respond to those who seek him.

HEBREWS 11:6 MSG

*E*verything is possible to the one who believes.

MARK 9:23 HCSB

*T*he ultimate response to Jesus' teaching
is belief and obedience.

JOHN MACARTHUR

Fear

* * *

Don't be afraid. God is for you.

BILLY GRAHAM

> Do not fear, for I am with you;
> do not be afraid, for I am your God.
>
> ISAIAH 41:10 HCSB

What have we to expect? Anything.
What have we to hope for? Everything.
What have we to fear? Nothing.

EDWARD B. PUSEY

The LORD is my light and my salvation—whom shall I fear?
The LORD is the stronghold of my life—of whom shall I be afraid?

PSALM 27:1 NIV

If a person fears God, he or she has no reason
to fear anything else. On the other hand, if a person
does not fear God, then fear becomes a way of life.

BETH MOORE

Enough

✽ ✽ ✽

You're blessed when you're content with just who you are—
no more, no less. That's the moment you find yourselves
proud owners of everything that can't be bought.

MATTHEW 5:5 MSG

The tiniest dewdrop hanging
from a grass blade in the morning
is big enough to reflect
the sunshine and the blue of the sky.

God isn't a talent scout looking for someone
who is "good enough" or "strong enough." He is looking
for someone with a heart set on Him, and He will do the rest.

VANCE HAVNER

I have God's more-than-enough,
More joy in one ordinary day
Than they get in all their shopping sprees.

PSALM 4:7 MSG

Time

Get reacquainted with God every day.

CRISWELL FREEMAN

Let us not become weary in doing good, for at the proper time we will reap a harvest if we do not give up.

GALATIANS 6:9 NIV

We all need to make time for God.
Even Jesus made time to be alone with the Father.

KAY ARTHUR

When the fullness of time had come, God sent forth His Son.

GALATIANS 4:4 NKJV

There is always enough time in a day to do God's will.

ROY LESSIN

I will praise the LORD
at all times;
His praise will always
be on my lips.

PSALM 34:1 HCSB

Hope

✻ ✻ ✻

*O*ptimism is the faith that leads to achievement.
Nothing can be done without hope and confidence.

HELEN KELLER

*B*e strong and let your heart take courage,
All you who hope in the LORD.

PSALM 31:24 NASB

*F*rom the little spark may burst a mighty flame.

DANTE

*M*ay the God of hope fill you
with all joy and peace
as you trust in Him,
so that you may overflow with hope.

ROMANS 15:13 NIV

*T*he three grand essentials of happiness are: something to do,
something to love, and something to hope for.

THOMAS CHALMERS

Beautiful World

*God has made everything
beautiful for its own time.
He has planted eternity
in the human heart.*

ECCLESIASTES 3:11 NLT

Experience God in the breathless wonder
and startling beauty that is all around you.
His sun shines warm upon your face.
His wind whispers in the treetops.

WENDY MOORE

As a countenance is made beautiful
by the soul's shining through it, so the world is beautiful
by the shining through it of God.

FRIEDRICH HEINRICH JACOBI

When one has once fully entered the realm of love, the
world—no matter how imperfect—becomes rich and beautiful,
for it consists solely of opportunities for love.

SØREN KIERKEGAARD

Real and Eternal

❀ ❀ ❀

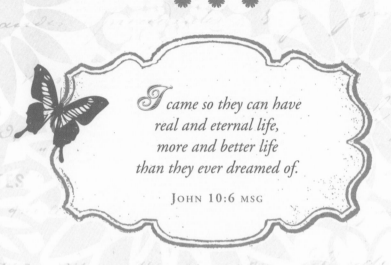

*I came so they can have
real and eternal life,
more and better life
than they ever dreamed of.*

JOHN 10:6 MSG

I am wholly His; I am peculiarly His;
I am universally His; I am eternally His.

THOMAS BENTON BROOKS

*F*or God so loved the world that he gave his
one and only Son, that whoever believes in him shall not perish
but have eternal life.

JOHN 3:16 NIV

*O*nly He who created the wonders of the world
entwines hearts in an eternal way.

I know exactly what his command produces: real and eternal
life. That's all I have to say. What the Father told me, I tell you.

JOHN 12:50 MSG

Be a Blessing

✿ ✿ ✿

God can pour on the blessings in astonishing ways
so that you're ready for anything and everything, more than just
ready to do what needs to be done.

2 CORINTHIANS 9:8 MSG

Having someone who understands
is a great blessing for ourselves. Being someone who understands
is a great blessing to others.

JANETTE OKE

The trustworthy person will get a rich reward.

PROVERBS 28:20 NLT

I thank God, my friend, for the blessing you are...
for the joy of your laughter...the comfort of your prayers...
the warmth of your smile.

*Bless—that's your job,
to bless.
You'll be a blessing
and also get a blessing.*

1 PETER 3:9 MSG

Our Prayers

* * *

$\mathscr{G}$od receives us just as we are and accepts our prayers
just as they are. In the same way that a small child cannot draw
a bad picture, so a child of God cannot offer a bad prayer.

RICHARD J. FOSTER

*$\mathscr{P}$rayer makes your heart bigger,
until it is capable
of containing the gift of God Himself.*

MOTHER TERESA

$\mathscr{D}$o your best and pray before you start.

JANA M.

$\mathscr{A}$ single grateful thought towards heaven
is the most perfect prayer.

G. E. LESSING

$\mathscr{K}$eep asking, and it will be given to you.
Keep searching, and you will find. Keep knocking,
and the door will be opened to you.

MATTHEW 7:7 HCSB

Every Kindness

∗ ∗ ∗

*The attitude of kindness
is everyday stuff like a great
pair of sneakers. Not frilly. Not fancy.
Just plain and comfortable.*

BARBARA JOHNSON

God can point to us in all future ages as examples of
the incredible wealth of his grace and kindness toward us,
as shown in all he has done for us
who are united with Christ Jesus.

EPHESIANS 2:7 NLT

Do all the good you can. By all the means you can. In all the
ways you can. In all the places you can. At all the times you can.
To all the people you can. As long as ever you can.

JOHN WESLEY

Let us be concerned about one another in order
to promote love and good works.

HEBREWS 10:24 HCSB

Careful Planning

* * *

*Careful planning puts you
ahead in the long run;
hurry and scurry
puts you further behind.*

PROVERBS 21:5 MSG

Most of us go through life praying a little,
planning a little, jockeying for position, hoping
but never being quite certain of anything, and always secretly
afraid that we will miss the way. This is a tragic waste of truth
and never gives rest to the heart. There is a better way....
Take instead the infinite wisdom of God.

A. W. TOZER

May he give you the desire of your heart
and make all your plans succeed.

PSALM 20:4 NIV

Thank You, Father, for the beautiful surprises
you are planning for me today.

ROBERT SCHULLER

The B-i-b-l-e

✳ ✳ ✳

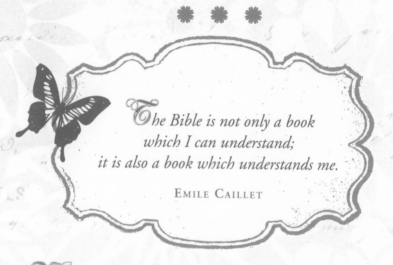

*The Bible is not only a book
which I can understand;
it is also a book which understands me.*

EMILE CAILLET

Your word is a lamp to guide my feet and a light for my path.

PSALM 119:105 NLT

Read the Bible so you can understand God
and know what to do.

JANA M.

God—His way is perfect;
the word of the LORD is pure.
He is a shield to all who take refuge in Him.

2 SAMUEL 22:31 HCSB

I've read the last page of the Bible.
It's going to turn out alright.

BILLY GRAHAM

Problems

✿ ✿ ✿

Let God's promises shine on your problems.

CORRIE TEN BOOM

Somewhere on the great world the sun is always shining,
and just so sure as you live, it will sometimes shine on you....
There is so much sunshine we must all have our share.

MYRTLE REED

I am about to do something new.
See, I have already begun! Do you not see it?
I will make a pathway through the wilderness.
I will create rivers in the dry wasteland.

ISAIAH 43:19 NLT

*Our heavenly Father
never takes anything
from His children unless
He means to give them
something better.*

GEORGE MUELLER

Courage

✽ ✽ ✽

Fear not, nor be dismayed; be strong, and of good courage.

JOSHUA 10:25 KJV

Courage is fear that has said its prayers.

KARL BARTH

Jesus spoke to them at once. "Don't be afraid," he said.
"Take courage. I am here!"

MATTHEW 14:27 NLT

Courage does not always roar. Sometimes courage
is the small, quiet voice at the end of the day saying,
"I will try again tomorrow."

MARY ANNE RADMACHER

Be strong and courageous!
Do not tremble or be dismayed,
for the LORD your God
is with you wherever you go.

JOSHUA 1:9 NASB

Love One Another

✽ ✽ ✽

Encourage one another and build up one another,
just as you also are doing.

1 THESSALONIANS 5:11 NASB

When you listen to your friends, when you encourage them,
when you do things their way (at least sometimes),
you're really telling them, "I'm glad you're my friend."

EMILIE BARNES

Love one another earnestly from a pure heart.

1 PETER 1:22 HCSB

There are high spots in all of our lives, and most of them come
about through encouragement from someone else.

GEORGE ADAMS

My command is this:
Love each other
as I have loved you.

JOHN 15:12 NIV

God's in Control

✤ ✤ ✤

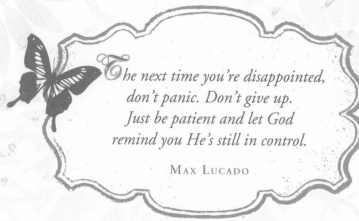

*The next time you're disappointed,
don't panic. Don't give up.
Just be patient and let God
remind you He's still in control.*

MAX LUCADO

Measure the size of the obstacles against the size of God.

BETH MOORE

[God] knows everything about us. And He cares
about everything. Moreover, He can manage every situation.
And He loves us!

HANNAH WHITALL SMITH

The LORD is my shepherd;
I have all that I need.
He lets me rest in green meadows;
he leads me beside peaceful streams.

PSALM 23:1–2 NLT

Forgive Others

�֍ ✤ ✤

Two persons will not be friends long if they cannot
forgive each other's little failings.

JEAN DE LA BRUYÈRE

Treat others the same way you want them to treat you.

LUKE 6:31 NASB

If you're going to forgive somebody eventually, why wait?

MARIE T. FREEMAN

If Jesus forgave those who nailed Him to the cross,
and if God forgives you and me, how can you withhold
your forgiveness from someone else?

ANNE GRAHAM LOTZ

*Be kind to one another, tenderhearted,
forgiving one another, even as God in Christ
forgave you.*

EPHESIANS 4:32 NKJV

Wear Love

Regardless of what else you put on, wear love.
It's your basic, all-purpose garment.
Never be without it.

COLOSSIANS 3:14 MSG

I have learned that to have a good friend is the purest of all God's gifts, for it is a love that has no exchange of payment.

FRANCES FARMER

Dear friends, let us love one another,
because love is from God, and everyone who loves
has been born of God and knows God.

1 JOHN 4:7 HCSB

Jesus, when we feel worthless, open us
to the warmth of Your love. Remind us that we are important
to the kingdom of God and loved for who we are.

MARILYN JANSEN

Do everything in love.

1 CORINTHIANS 16:14 NIV

Rejoice

* * *

You can complain because roses have thorns,
or you can rejoice because thorns have roses.

TOM WILSON

Always be full of joy in the Lord. I say it again—rejoice!

PHILIPPIANS 4:4 NLT

The highest and most desirable state of the soul
is to praise God in celebration for being alive.

LUCI SWINDOLL

My heart rejoices, and I praise Him with my song.

PSALM 28:7 HCSB

*This is the day
which the LORD has made;
Let us rejoice
and be glad in it.*

PSALM 118:24 NASB

A Song

✿ ✿ ✿

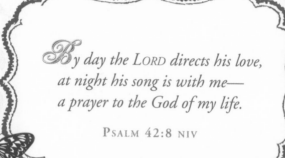

*By day the LORD directs his love,
at night his song is with me—
a prayer to the God of my life.*

PSALM 42:8 NIV

A friend hears the song in my heart and sings it to me
when my memory fails.

PIONEER GIRLS LEADERS' HANDBOOK

*S*ing to the LORD, you His faithful ones,
and praise His holy name.

PSALM 30:4 HCSB

I breathed a song into the air;
It fell to earth, I know not where...
And the song, from beginning to end,
I found again in the heart of a friend.

HENRY WADSWORTH LONGFELLOW

Words

* * *

A little kindly advice is better than a great deal of scolding.

FANNY CROSBY

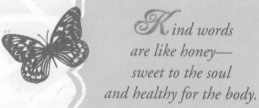

*Kind words
are like honey—
sweet to the soul
and healthy for the body.*

PROVERBS 16:24 NLT

*E*veryone should be quick to listen,
slow to speak and slow to become angry.

JAMES 1:19 NIV

A friend understands what you are trying to say...
even when your thoughts aren't fitting into words.

ANN D. PARRISH

*M*ay the words of my mouth
and the meditation of my heart
be pleasing to you,
O LORD, my rock and my redeemer.

PSALM 19:14 NLT

Be Joyful

* * *

*My soul shall be joyful
in the LORD:
it shall rejoice
in his salvation.*

PSALM 35:9 KJV

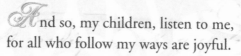

*And so, my children, listen to me,
for all who follow my ways are joyful.*

PROVERBS 8:32 NLT

Life need not be easy to be joyful. Joy is not
the absence of trouble, but the presence of Christ.

WILLIAM VANDERHOVEN

How necessary it is to cultivate a spirit of joy....
To act lovingly is to begin to feel loving,
and certainly to act joyfully brings joy to others,
which in turn makes one feel joyful.

DOROTHY DAY

My Purpose

* * *

For we are God's masterpiece. He has created us
anew in Christ Jesus, so we can do the good things
he planned for us long ago.

EPHESIANS 2:10 NLT

Do what you know best: if you're a runner, run;
if you're a bell, ring.

IGNAS BERNSTEIN

O LORD, you are our Father.
We are the clay, you are the potter;
we are all the work of your hand.

ISAIAH 64:8 NIV

*Remember that you are needed.
There is at least
one important work to be done
that will not be done unless you do it.*

CHARLES ALLEN

Strength

✽ ✽ ✽

*I*t is strength that endures the unendurable and spills over into joy, thanking the Father who makes us strong enough to take part in everything bright and beautiful that he has for us.

COLOSSIANS 1:11–12 MSG

*B*e strong in your faith. Remember that your Christian brothers and sisters all over the world are going through the same kind of suffering you are.

1 PETER 5:9 NLT

*T*he joy of Jesus will be my strength—it will be in my heart. Every person I meet will see it in my work, my walk, my prayer— in everything.

MOTHER TERESA

*T*he LORD is
my strength and shield.
I trust him
with all my heart.

PSALM 28:7 NLT

Generosity

Give, and it will be given to you. A good measure,
pressed down, shaken together and running over,
will be poured into your lap. For with the measure you use,
it will be measured to you.

LUKE 6:38 NIV

The measure of a life, after all,
is not its duration but its donation.

CORRIE TEN BOOM

Give freely and spontaneously. Don't have
a stingy heart. The way you handle matters like this
triggers GOD, your God's, blessing in everything you do,
all your work and ventures.... Always be generous,
open purse and hands, give to your neighbors in trouble.

DEUTERONOMY 15:10–11 MSG

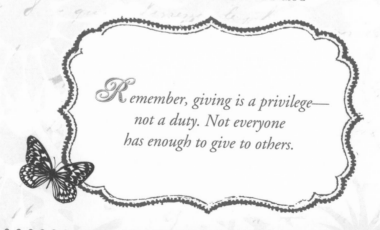

*Remember, giving is a privilege—
not a duty. Not everyone
has enough to give to others.*

Keep Trying

✿ ✿ ✿

The glory is not in never failing,
but in rising every time you fail.

CHINESE PROVERB

The LORD directs the steps of the godly. He delights
in every detail of their lives. Though they stumble,
they will never fall, for the LORD holds them by the hand.

PSALM 37:23–24 NLT

You may have to fight the battle more than once to win it.

MARGARET THATCHER

Take the old prophets as your mentors.
They put up with anything, went through everything,
and never once quit, all the time honoring God.

JAMES 5:10–11 MSG

*The Lord loves us—
perhaps most of all—
when we fail and try again.*

EMILIE GRIFFIN

What We Need

* * *

God is always sufficient in perfect proportion to our need.

BETH MOORE

Let us then approach the throne of grace with confidence,
so that we may receive mercy and find grace
to help us in our time of need.

HEBREWS 4:16 NIV

What God sends is almost always better than what we ask for,
but even if it isn't, it is always what we need.

MARILYN JANSEN

Don't worry about anything; instead, pray about everything.
Tell God what you need, and thank him for all he has done.

PHILIPPIANS 4:6 NLT

What God gives in answer
to our prayers will always be
the thing we most urgently need,
and it will always be sufficient.

ELISABETH ELLIOT

Humbly

> *Let another praise you, and not your own mouth;*
> *someone else, and not your own lips.*
>
> PROVERBS 27:2 NIV

Everything which relates to God is infinite. We must therefore, while we keep our hearts humble, keep our aims high.

HANNAH MORE

Everyone who exalts himself will be humbled, and he who humbles himself will be exalted.

LUKE 14:11 NASB

Our self-distrust, while keeping us humble, must not cloud the joy with which we lean on our faithful covenant God.

J. I. PACKER

What does the LORD require of you
But to do justice, to love kindness,
And to walk humbly with your God?

MICAH 6:8 NASB

You Can Do It

* * *

*If you think you can, you can.
And if you think you can't, you're right.*

MARY KAY ASH

Be strong and do not lose courage,
for there is reward for your work.

2 CHRONICLES 15:7 NASB

God has always used ordinary people
to carry out His extraordinary mission.

Greater is He who is in you than he who is in the world.

1 JOHN 4:4 NASB

There is no one giant step that does it. It's a lot of little steps.

PETER A. COHEN

I know you can do it. I've seen you do harder stuff!

EMILY P.

Serve Others

* * *

If you aren't serving, you're just existing,
because life is meant for ministry.

RICK WARREN

Yes indeed, it is good when you obey the royal law as found
in the Scriptures: "Love your neighbor as yourself."

JAMES 2:8 NLT

In everything I did, I showed you that
by this kind of hard work we must help the weak,
remembering the words the Lord Jesus himself said:
"It is more blessed to give than to receive."

ACTS 20:35 NIV

*I have discovered
that when I please Christ,
I end up inadvertently serving others
far more effectively.*

BETH MOORE

Wait

✿ ✿ ✿

In times of uncertainty, wait. Always, if you have any doubt, wait. Do not force yourself to any action. If you have a restraint in your spirit, wait until all is clear, and do not go against it.

MRS. CHARLES E. COWMAN

Don't trap yourself by making a rash promise to God and only later counting the cost.

PROVERBS 20:25 NLT

Waiting is the hardest kind of work, but God knows best, and we may joyfully leave all in His hands.

Wait for the LORD;
be strong and take heart
and wait for the LORD.

PSALM 27:14 NIV

By His wisdom, He orders His delays so that they prove to be far better than our hurries.

C. H. SPURGEON

Trust Steadily

✺ ✺ ✺

*L*ife is not easy for any of us. But what of that?
We must have perseverance and...confidence in ourselves.
We must believe that we are gifted for something
and that this thing must be attained.

MARIE CURIE

*L*ead me by your truth and teach me,
for you are the God who saves me.
All day long I put my hope in you.

PSALM 25:5 NLT

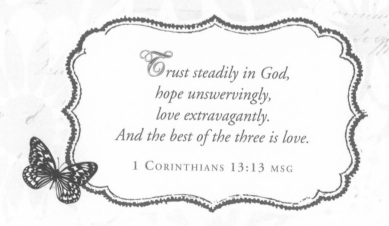

*T*rust steadily in God,
hope unswervingly,
love extravagantly.
And the best of the three is love.

1 CORINTHIANS 13:13 MSG

*L*ife is not meant to be easy, my child;
but take courage—it can be delightful.

GEORGE BERNARD SHAW

Attitude

✽ ✽ ✽

*D*eveloping a positive attitude means working continually to find what is uplifting and encouraging.

BARBARA JOHNSON

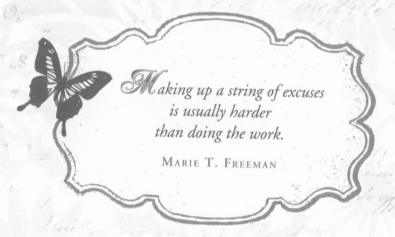

*M*aking up a string of excuses
is usually harder
than doing the work.

MARIE T. FREEMAN

*K*eep vigilant watch over your heart;
that's where life starts.
Don't talk out of both sides of your mouth;
avoid careless banter, white lies, and gossip.
Keep your eyes straight ahead;
ignore all sideshow distractions.

PROVERBS 4:23–25 MSG

*R*eplace your excuses with fresh determination.

CHARLES SWINDOLL

Every Good Work

* * *

Where there are no good works, there is no faith.
If works and love do not blossom forth, it is not genuine faith,
the gospel has not yet gained a foothold,
and Christ is not yet rightly known.

MARTIN LUTHER

I tell you the truth, anyone who believes in me will do
the same works I have done, and even greater works,
because I am going to be with the Father.

JOHN 14:12 NLT

Faith...has sustained me—faith in the God of the Bible,
a God, as someone once put it, not small enough
to be understood but big enough to be worshiped.

ELISABETH ELLIOT

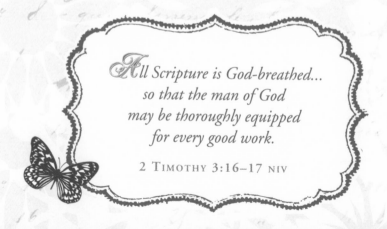

All Scripture is God-breathed...
so that the man of God
may be thoroughly equipped
for every good work.

2 TIMOTHY 3:16–17 NIV

Enthusiasm

* * *

You are the recipient of Christ's sacrificial love.
Accept it enthusiastically and share it fervently.
Jesus deserves your enthusiasm; the world deserves it;
and you deserve the experience of sharing it.

Love the Lord your God, walk in all his ways,
obey his commands, hold firmly to him, and serve him
with all your heart and all your soul.

JOSHUA 22:5 NLT

We act as though comfort and luxury were the chief
requirements of life, when all we need to make us really happy
is something to be enthusiastic about.

CHARLES KINGSLEY

Never be lazy, but work hard
and serve the Lord enthusiastically.

ROMANS 12:11 NLT

Wildly Wonderful

✼ ✼ ✼

What a wildly wonderful world, GOD!
You made it all, with Wisdom at your side,
made earth overflow with your wonderful creations.

PSALM 104:24 MSG

I still find each day too short for all the thoughts
I want to think, all the walks I want to take, all the books
I want to read, and all the friends I want to see.
The longer I live, the more my mind dwells upon
the beauty and the wonder of the world.

JOHN BURROUGHS

You have done such wonderful things.
Who can compare with you, O God?

PSALM 71:19 NLT

O God, great and wonderful,
who has created the heavens,
dwelling in the light and beauty of it...
teach me to praise You.

ISIDORE OF SEVILLE

Ellie Claire™ Gift & Paper Corp.
Minneapolis, MN 55438
www.ellieclaire.com

God's Promises for a Girl's Heart

Journal
© 2011 by Ellie Claire Gift & Paper Corp.

ISBN 978-1-60936-130-3

Compiled by Marilyn Jansen
Cover and interior design by Jeff and Lisa Franke.

Printed in China.